This journal
belongs to

....

....

Date

....

Ellie Claire® Gift & Paper Expressions
Franklin, TN 37067 | EllieClaire.com
Ellie Claire is a registered trademark of Worthy Media, Inc.

The Illustrated Word Coloring Journal
© 2017 Museum of the Bible, Washington, DC 20024
For more information about the Museum of the Bible, visit museumoftheBible.org.

Published by Ellie Claire, an imprint of Worthy Publishing Group, a division of Worthy Media, Inc.,
in association with Museum of the Bible.

ISBN 978-1-945470-19-6

Stock or custom editions of Ellie Claire titles may be purchased in bulk for educational, business, ministry,
fund-raising, or sales promotional use. For information, please e-mail info@EllieClaire.com

Development, interior design, and typesetting by Hudson Bible.
Illustrations by Ekaterina Vitkovskaya
Cover design by Jeff Jansen | AestheticSoup.net

Printed in China

1 2 3 4 5 6 7 8 9 – RRD – 21 20 19 18 17

Oh give thanks
to the
LORD,
for he is good.

1 CHRONICLES 16:34 ESV

Hours and Psalter of Elizabeth de Bohun, Countess of Northampton | 1330-1340

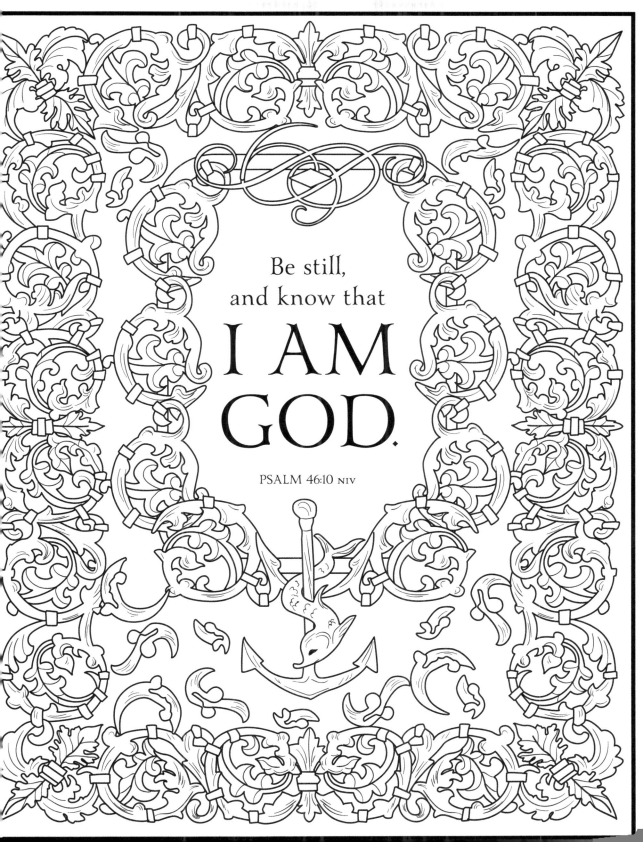

Be still,
and know that

I AM
GOD.

PSALM 46:10 NIV

Hours and Psalter of Elizabeth de Bohun, Countess of Northampton | c. 1350

Whoever pursues RIGHTEOUSNESS
and KINDNESS will find

LIFE & HONOR.

PROVERBS 21:21 NRSV

Natural Parchment Esther Scroll Without Rollers | Israel, 2000s

Natural Parchment Esther Scroll Without Rollers | Israel, 2000s

Martin Luther: Das Newe Testament Deutsch,
Woodcuts by Melchior Lotter d.J. | Wittenberg, 1522

Old Parchment Esther Scroll, Illustrated | Israel, c. 1950

The LORD
bless you and
KEEP YOU.

NUMBERS 6:24 NIV

Ethiopic Manuscript | c. 1750

Psalter in the German Translation of Martin Luther, with Kurzen Summarien und
Gebetlein für die Hausüeter unnd ihre Kinder, by Nicolaus Selneccer | 1592

TRUST

in the LORD, and do

GOOD.

PSALM 37:3 NKJV

Natural Parchment Esther Scroll Without Rollers | Israel, 2000s

ני לא תוכל לו כי בֹּ
בּרים עָמוּ וסָרִיסִי ה
הָמָן אֶל הַמִּשְׁתֶּה
וְהָמָן כִּשְׁתּוֹת עֵם

Natural Parchment Esther Scroll With Wooden Handle | Bohemia, 1500s

May the Lord bless
his people with

PEACE!

PSALM 29:11 ESV

Litany from Book of Common Prayer, for the Use of the Church of All Saints,
with Carved Wooden Board Cover | 1981

Natural Parchment Esther Scroll Inside a Silver Case | Israel, 1930's

I KNOW
THAT MY
REDEEMER
LIVES.

JOB 19:25 NIV

HESTO LIBRB EP
qual flapla lappealiplit traum libry:
telutinta fcrpaira fedic leggre zaldire
cungramco melew et arliegqone pa
arezone. C laprimarzzziii eparete
inloprimo capriote ezquicte libre e
firavanl brzatin deleze corin ercalte
leparole aqtexta erotiqui capiecte nine
frirque er algum. zere liberi trzabriun

Ethiopic Manuscript | c. 1750

Martin Luther: Das Newe Testament Deutsch,
Woodcuts by Melchior Lotter d.J. | Wittenberg, 1522

Very Fine Parchment Esther Scroll Without Rollers | Israel, 2000s

Litany from Book of Common Prayer, for the Use of the Church of All Saints,
with Carved Wooden Board Cover | 1981

The LORD
is my
ROCK,
my
FORTRESS
and my
DELIVERER.

PSALM 18:2 NIV

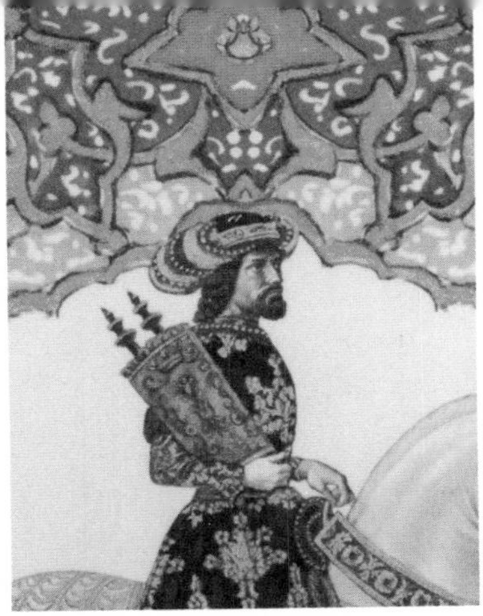

Old Parchment Esther Scroll, Illustrated | Israel, c. 1950

Martin Luther: Das Newe Testament Deutsch,
Woodcuts by Melchior Lotter d.J. | Wittenberg, 1522

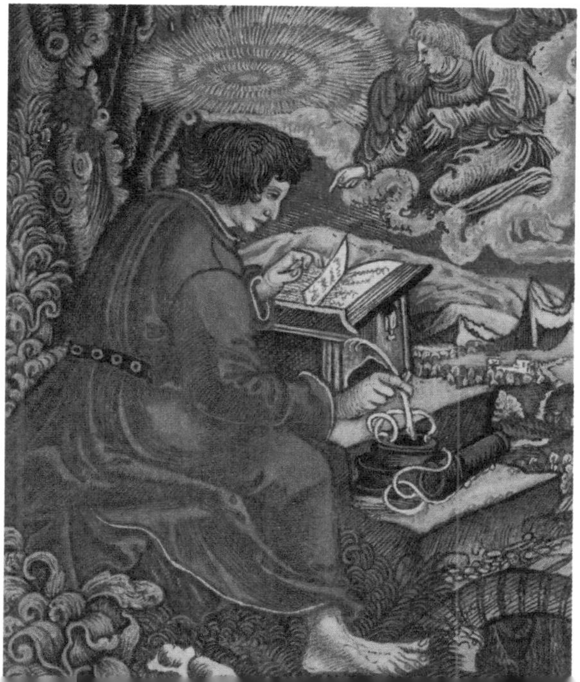

Psalter in the German Translation of Martin Luther, with Kurzen Summarien und
Gebetlein für die Hausüeter unnd ihre Kinder, by Nicolaus Selneccer | 1592

I will dwell
in the house
of the LORD

FOREVER.

PSALM 23:6 NIV

Hours and Psalter of Elizabeth de Bohun, Countess of Northampton | 1330-1340

Litany from Book of Common Prayer, for the Use of the Church of All Saints,
with Carved Wooden Board Cover | 1981

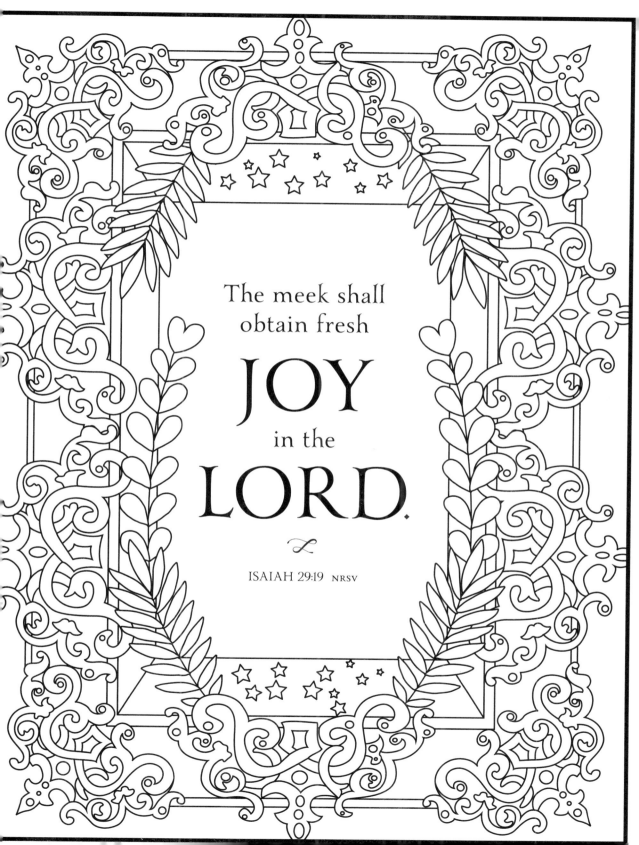

The meek shall
obtain fresh

JOY

in the

LORD.

ISAIAH 29:19 NRSV

Christ, have mercy upon us.
Lord, have mercy upon us.
Lord, have mercy upon us.
Then shall the Priest, and the people with him, say the Lord's Prayer.

Our Father, which art in heaven, Hallowed be thy Name. Thy kingdom come. Thy will be done in earth as it is in heaven. Give us this day our daily bread. And forgive us our trespasses, as we forgive them that trespass against us. And lead us not into temptation; But deliver us from evil. Amen.

O Lord, deal not with us after our sins.
Neither reward us after our iniquities.
Let us pray.

O God, merciful Father, that despisest not the sighing of a contrite heart, nor the desire of such as be sorrowful; Mercifully assist our prayers that we make before thee in all our troubles and adversities, whensoever they oppress us; and graciously hear us, that those evils, which the craft & subtilty of the devil or man worketh against us, be brought to nought; and by the providence of thy goodness they may be dispersed; that we thy servants, hurt by no persecutions

Hours and Psalter of Elizabeth de Bohun, Countess of Northampton | 1330-1340

Gospel Book, in Ge'ez | 1900s

Martin Luther: Das Newe Testament Deutsch,
Woodcuts by Melchior Lotter d.J | Wittenberg, 1522

Natural Parchment Esther Scroll Without Rollers | Israel, 2000s

Natural Parchment Esther Scroll Without Rollers | Israel, late 1900s

Natural Parchment Esther Scroll With Wooden Handle | Bohemia, 1500s

Litany from Book of Common Prayer, for the Use of the Church of All Saints,
with Carved Wooden Board Cover | 1981

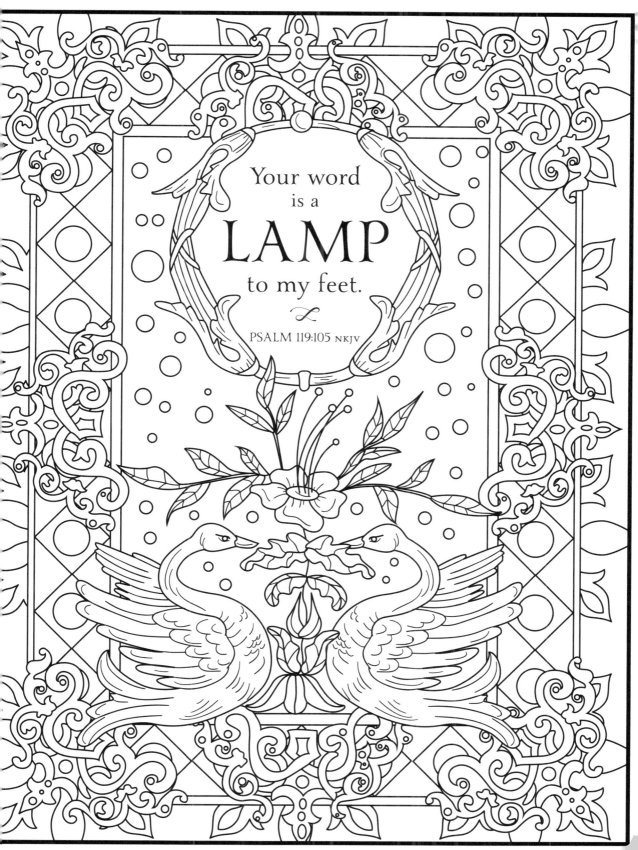

Your word
is a
LAMP
to my feet.

PSALM 119:105 NKJV

Martin Luther: Das Newe Testament Deutsch,
Woodcuts by Melchior Lotter d.J. | Wittenberg, 1522

Very Fine Parchment Esther Scroll Without Rollers | Israel, 2000s

Bible in Latin; Johann Fust and Peter Schoeffer | Mainz, 1462

LORD
MY GOD,
I will
PRAISE
you forever.

PSALM 30:12 NIV

Hattem Vulgate | c. 1420–1430

Our God is full of
COMPASSION.

PSALM 116:5 NIV

Psalter for the Use of Brussels, Beginning of Psalm 1 | Northern France, c. 1260

Armenian Illuminated Gospel Book | Cilicia (southern Turkey), 12th century text,
with illuminations by the artist Ghazar added in the 14th century

Hours and Psalter of Elizabeth de Bohun, Countess of Northampton | c. 1330-1340

Fear not,

for I AM

WITH YOU.

ISAIAH 43:5 NKJV

Natural Parchment Esther Scroll Without Rollers | Israel, 2000s